REMEMBER: LEADER GUIDE

Remember
God's Covenants and the Cross

Remember
978-1-7910-3020-9
978-1-7910-3021-6 *eBook*

Remember: DVD
978-1-7910-3019-3

Remember: Leader Guide
978-1-7910-3022-3
978-1-7910-3018-6 *eBook*

Also by Susan Robb

Called: Hearing and Responding to God's Voice

Seven Words: Listening to Christ from the Cross

The Angels of Christmas: Hearing God's Voice in Advent

On Purpose: Finding God's Voice in Your Passion
(With Magrey R. de Vega, Sam McGlothlin, and Jevon Caldwell-Gross)

REMEMBER

God's Covenants
and the Cross

SUSAN ROBB

ABINGDON PRESS | NASHVILLE

Remember:
God's Covenants and the Cross
Leader Guide

Copyright © 2023 Abingdon Press
All rights reserved.

978-1-7910-3022-3

Scripture quotations are taken from the New Revised Standard Version, Updated Edition (NRSVue). Copyright © 2021 National Council of Churches of Christ in the United States of America. Used by permission. All rights reserved worldwide.

MANUFACTURED IN THE UNITED STATES OF AMERICA

CONTENTS

About the
Leader Guide Writer

Randy Horick is a freelance writer
who lives in Nashville, Tennessee.

INTRODUCTION

In *Remember: God's Covenants and the Cross*, Susan Robb takes an unconventional approach to a Lenten study—focusing not just on the events in the days leading up to Jesus's entry into Jerusalem, arrest, execution, and resurrection, but on the long sweep of God's history with God's people.

Upon further examination, however, this approach makes a great deal of biblical sense, particularly when you recall the Scriptures we often study during the Advent season. Lessons and Carols services, a favorite among many congregations, traditionally begin with a reading from Genesis about the fall of Adam and Eve. Luke's Gospel traces Jesus's genealogy to those first humans, while Matthew goes back to Abraham the patriarch. Scripture readings during Advent draw heavily on the Old Testament prophets. John's Gospel begins with a reminder of God's activity in creation: "In the beginning."

As Robb notes in *Remember: God's Covenants and the Cross*, "the rituals and Scriptures of these seasons helps us better understand the Incarnation, Resurrection, and our own salvation history." That's how covenants connect to memory. In the beginning, God sought an intimate relationship with human beings based on trust and faith. When people broke that relationship early on, the Scriptures recount our entire "salvation history"—God's efforts to reach people, to remind them of God's love and compassion, and to guide them back toward the relationship that God always desired.

Each of the covenants you will study in this book—beginning with Noah and continuing with Abraham, Moses, and the children of Israel, through David and beyond—is a landmark in this salvation history. Just as landmarks help us remember where we are in a journey to a familiar destination, God's covenants are not just promises about what is ahead; they are reminders of where we have been, and of God's love and faithfulness that persist, that seek to find a way to return us to an Edenic state with God, in the wake of continued demonstrations of human failing and faithlessness.

In this book, Robb invites us to look more deeply at each of these encounters with God and God's promises. She notes how God not only makes promises to the covenant participants but reminds them of God's past demonstrations of love and deliverance. As she points out, the covenant with Noah and creation comes after God has delivered Noah and re-created the world. Along Abraham's faith journey, God reminds him not only of the promise that he will be the father of a great nation but of how God has walked with him along the way. The covenant with Moses and the children of Israel at Sinai comes after God has rescued them from Egypt—an act they were called to remember from that time on. God makes a covenant with David after God has elevated him from an obscure shepherd boy and chosen him as the king of the nation. In the time of Jeremiah, the promise of a new covenant written on human hearts comes after the people are called to remember how utterly they had turned away from God.

This salvation history culminates in the events recounted in the final chapters of the Gospels. Notably, in their last meal together, Jesus speaks to his disciples about how the wine they are sharing represents his blood of the covenant. In addition to covenant language, he invokes the role of memory when he tells them: "Do this, as often as you drink it, in remembrance of me" (1 Corinthians 11:25).

In that moment, Jesus's disciples may not yet grasp what they are called to remember. After all, Jesus is still with them. He has not yet been arrested and crucified. But in the days to come, after they have encountered the risen Christ, they come to understand. In the ultimate covenant attempt to bring God and human beings back into the relationship God desires, the Word—the mind and spirit of God—became fully human and suffered a brutal human death. As in so many of the other covenant stories in this book, God acted unilaterally; Jesus's death and resurrection were not contingent upon human faithfulness in the way that two parties must keep the obligations of a formal contract.

Instead, we remember that Jesus prayed for the forgiveness of his killers even as he was being killed. When we share Communion together, we remember the depth of Jesus's love that led him to pour himself out on our behalf. We also are called to remember that we, as Jesus's disciples, are to love fearlessly and faithfully without counting the cost—because we also remember that the cross is not the end. Instead, it is the final landmark on our way home. We can come to the cross without fear because we know where it leads. We remember.

This Leader Guide is designed to help Christian adult education leaders guide a group through a six-session Lenten study of the covenants and remembrance, a study informed by Robb's book. The guide contains quotes from her book that can serve as prompts for discussion, but groups will gain the most when the guide is accompanied by both reading *Remember: God's Covenants and the Cross* and the accompanying Scriptures.

About the Sessions

Here is an overview of the six sessions in this Leader Guide:

- In session one, "Noah: God's Covenant with Creation," participants will connect God's regret over what creation had become to God's effort to re-create the world rather than to destroy it and walk away forever. They will recognize how God connects covenants with memory, through the sign of the bow that God places in the sky. They will experience some of the sense of wonder that Noah and his family must have felt in seeing that first, miraculous rainbow. And they will see in God's re-creation their own call to forgive, to reconcile, and to participate in the healing of the world.

- In session two, "Abraham: A Promise of Nations," participants will connect Abraham's willingness to step into the new and unknown with their own spiritual journey. They will gain a deeper understanding of what it means to "walk by faith and not by sight" or by previous experience. In confronting

Abraham's own times of doubt and wandering, they will more fully appreciate how God remains faithful to covenants even when we fall away in our own lives.

- Session three, "Moses and Israel: Words of Life and Freedom," takes participants along with Moses and the children of Israel to the foot of Mount Sinai. In sharing this journey, they will gain a deeper appreciation of how God's covenant was not about arbitrary rules mandated by an all-powerful being but an invitation to experience abundant life in a community that is in a harmonious relationship with God.

- In session four, "David: An Eternal Covenant," participants will place themselves in the position of those who first understood God's promise to David as an eternal covenant with the Jewish people. They will consider how those words would have been understood in David's time and by people of subsequent generations who remembered God's deliverance, God's elevation of the lowly and unpretentious, and God's faithfulness across the centuries. Then they will apply this understanding to gain a deeper appreciation of what God's covenant with David means for Christians, who understand Jesus as both the fulfillment of God's promise to continue David's line and the restoration of the original ideal of God as the true king over God's people.

- In session five, "From Jeremiah to Jesus: The Covenant of the Heart," participants will understand God's actions through the prophet Jeremiah in light of the utter rebellion against God' s love and justice that the people have committed. They will recognize how this rebellion came to be associated with our image of hell—a place not created by God for punishment but as a construct of human beings choosing to separate themselves from God. Against this backdrop, participants will recognize the astounding depth of God's love and commitment to an intimate relationship with humans, as expressed in

Jeremiah's announcement of a new covenant that God will write on the hearts of the people.

- In session six, "Jesus and the New Covenant," participants will place themselves in the position of the disciples who gathered with Jesus for what they would later remember as their final meal together. They will connect Jesus's language, in which he says his blood represents a renewal of the covenant, with previous covenants. They will understand his invitation to act "in remembrance of me" as a call to remember what Jesus is about to do as a model for self-giving love and to understand the cross, like the rainbow in the time of Noah, as an eternal sign that human death and violence have no power to prevent God's love from reaching us—or to prevent us from coming home at last to God.

Each of the six session plans includes:

- Stated goals for you to keep in mind as you lead discussions.
- The printed text, from the New Revised Standard Version, Updated Edition (NRSVue), that serves to frame the discussion of each session. (Sessions contain additional Scripture texts as well, and all sessions refer participants to other passages in several discussion questions.)
- Extensive discussion questions to facilitate participants' engagement with both the biblical text and *Remember: God's Covenants and the Cross* book. You likely won't have time or desire to use all of the questions; choose the ones most interesting and/or relevant to your group.
- Opening and closing prayers to ground your sessions in an atmosphere of worship.

Some sessions contain optional, easy-to-prepare, and easy-to-do-activities to serve as "icebreakers" or interactive introductions to the session's topic. Each session's Suggested Leader Preparation notes will alert you to any extra materials or preparation you need.

May God, in great grace, use this guide and your group's study to draw you closer to the cross—and to Jesus's words to you.

SESSION ONE

Noah:

God's Covenant with Creation

Session Goals

This session's reading, discussion, reflection, and prayer will equip participants to:

- Understand the various types of covenants presented in Scripture and their meaning;
- Connect covenants and communal memory;
- Understand God's covenant with creation as an attempt to re-create the world and enter into a more harmonious relationship with human beings;
- Recognize our own role in and claim responsibility for working toward the healing and repair of the world.

Biblical Foundations

Then God said to Noah and to his sons with him, "As for me, I am establishing my covenant with you and your descendants after you and with every living creature that is with you, the birds, the domestic animals, and every animal of the earth with you, as many as came out of the ark. I establish my covenant with you, that never again shall all flesh be cut off by the waters of a flood, and never again shall there be a flood to destroy the earth." God said, "This is the sign of the covenant that I make between me and you and every living creature that is with you, for all future generations: I have set my bow in the clouds, and it shall be a sign of the covenant between me and the earth. When I bring clouds over the earth and the bow is seen in the clouds, I will remember my covenant that is between me and you and every living creature of all flesh; and the waters shall never again become a flood to destroy all flesh. When the bow is in the clouds, I will see it and remember the everlasting covenant between God and every living creature of all flesh that is on the earth." God said to Noah, "This is the sign of the covenant that I have established between me and all flesh that is on the earth."

(Genesis 9:8-17)

Suggested Leader Preparation

- Before your first session, set aside enough time to read the entire account of Noah and the Flood (Genesis 6:5–9:29). Read these passages in more than one translation (for example, New Revised Standard Version, Updated Edition, New International Version, New American Bible Revised Edition, The Message), including one you've never read before. Read these chapters aloud. Try summarizing the passage in your own words.

- As background, read the story of Creation in Genesis 1 and 2. Again, try reading this passage in several translations. Make notes comparing God's view of completed creation and God's view at the time of Noah.

- Carefully read Remember: God's Covenants and the Cross by Robb, the introduction and chapter one. Note any material you need or want to research further before the session.

- Have on hand Bible dictionaries and concordances (and/ or identify trusted online equivalents) and a variety of Bible translations for participants to use (recommended), and pencils/pens and paper. If you are in touch with the people likely to join you for these sessions, invite them to bring their own Bibles. Optional: Gather an assortment of recent newspapers and magazines.

- If using the DVD (also available as streaming video) in your study, preview the session one segment and choose the best time in your session to view it.

As Your Group Gathers:
Orient the Study toward Covenants and Memory

Welcome participants. Ask them to introduce themselves and to talk briefly about what they hope to gain from this study of Robb's *Remember: God's Covenants and the Cross*. Be ready to talk about your personal interest in and hopes for the study as well. If no one mentions Lent specifically, ask participants why they chose to be part of a Lenten study. Invite them to discuss various ways in which they have observed Lent, both personally and as part of a faith community.

Ask:

- What do we remember during Lent? Why do we make this part of our memory as followers of Jesus?
- How does our memory of the events of Jesus's journey to the cross connect to God's promises to us? to God's faithfulness?
- How does Lent connect to God's attempts throughout history to restore a relationship with human beings based on faith and trust?

Emphasize that this is not only a Lenten study; it is about the entire salvation story that is presented in the Bible. Note that, while for Christians today Lent is a time when we reflect on Jesus's journey to the cross, we must go all the way back to Genesis to appreciate fully God's faithfulness toward fallible and faithless human beings—and God's desire to be in intimate relationship to us.

Pray this prayer or one in your own words:

O God, let this season for us be more than a casual or routine remembrance of the depth of your love for us. Prepare us to do more than give up some small part of our daily routine in observance of Jesus's sacrifice. Help us to understand the history of your love for us that has manifested itself since you created this world. And help us to trust in your promises so that we may fearlessly follow Jesus all the way to the cross, knowing that the cross for us is not the end but a symbol of your unending love for us—a love that triumphs over this world. Amen.

Frame the Study around Covenants

In the first sentence of the introduction to her book, Robb writes "This book explores the relationship between Lent and memory (God's and our own), and especially the season's connection to the covenants in the Bible." That's a good place to begin this conversation. For many Christians (if not most), there's no clear connection between covenants that begin with Noah and Abraham and Lent, the season in which we reflect on Jesus's sacrifice and on our own call to take up our cross and follow him. During Lent, we don't typically make a point of remembering God's promise to creation after the Flood, or God's covenant with Abraham. To start the discussion, invite participants to share what, if any, connections they see between the cross and some of the covenants discussed in this book:

- Noah and God's covenant with creation
- God's covenant with Abraham
- God's covenant with the Israelite people through Moses
- God's covenant with David

Continuing the conversation, note Robb's emphasis on our salvation history, or what some call the salvation story—the story of how God repeatedly and relentlessly works to bring creation and humankind back into the harmonious relationship that God always desired and intended. The story culminates in the life, death, and resurrection of Jesus. But as Robb argues, the narratives of God's people that begin with Adam and Eve and run through the Resurrection are not a group of separate stories but one unbroken story.

Discuss:

- Why would God repeatedly try to restore broken relationships with rebellious humans?
- Why would a God with the power to speak the world into existence even need to try repeatedly to draw human beings back into a harmonious relationship?

What's a Covenant, Anyway?
And Why Covenants?

As Robb explains, covenants are a primary motif in Hebrew and Christian Scriptures and a primary way that God reaches out to humanity. Let's look a little more closely at what these covenants involve. Discuss:

- What kinds of agreements come to mind when you think of covenants?
- How do divine covenants in the Bible differ from human covenants?
- Why do you think some covenants between God and humans involve mutual promises, while others are unilateral on God's part?
- Why would God choose to reach out to humanity through covenants as a way to prove God's sincerity and faithfulness in providing what's best for God's children and all of creation?
- What do covenants have to do with remembering? Think of examples of secular covenants in our own contemporary society that call on us to "remember."
- How does memory play into our relationship with God?
- How does it play into the relationship between God's people and God as revealed through Scripture?

The Broken World

As Robb notes in taking the story back to Adam and Eve in the garden of Eden, the relationship between God and human beings quickly becomes broken, leading to the disaster in the time of Noah. Use the questions below to discuss how the original relationship became so broken and how God responded to it.

- Reread Genesis 3:1–4:16. How would you describe the original relationship between God and the first human beings?

- Although there is no formal covenant between God and Adam and Eve, there was a relationship that appeared to be based on mutual understanding. How would you describe that understanding?
- What led that relationship to become broken?
- How does God respond to the failure of Adam and Eve to trust in God fully?
- Have there been times when you experienced a lack of trust in God? How was your relationship affected?
- By the time of Noah, the break between God and human beings has deteriorated much further. Why, in your opinion, would God take such a drastic step as to "reboot" creation through the Flood?
- Why would God promise Noah and creation not to destroy the world again by flood? Why would God foreclose this possibility, given what God has seen of human behavior?
- Is it conceivable that this was in some ways a "learning experience" for God? If so, how?
- Where have you encountered brokenness in this world? How do you respond to this brokenness?
- How do your experiences with brokenness contribute to your understanding of God's reaction to the world of Noah's time?

The Sign of the Rainbow

Robb emphasizes that the symbol of the rainbow, placed deliberately by God in the sky, was meant to serve as a permanent reminder of God's covenant with creation—repurposing the image of an instrument of war into an affirmation of God's love for the world. Invite the participants to discuss these questions:

- When have you ever been awestruck by a rainbow? Can you describe the experience? What was so striking about it?
- What are the terms of the covenant God makes with Noah and creation? What are the obligations of Noah and his descendants?

- What does it mean to you that "God remembered Noah" as he and his family and the animals rode out the Flood on the ark?
- What does the rainbow signify in this story? How does it connect to remembering for God? How does it connect to remembering for us?
- When have you found a sign that reminded you that you were important to and loved by God?

Robb connects the rainbow to the sign of the cross. She also points out how the sign of the cross symbolizes different emphases in the Catholic and Protestant traditions.

- What does the symbol of Jesus on the cross represent to you?
- What does the symbol of the empty cross represent to you?
- How does the self-imposed limits on God's power in God's covenant with creation connect you to the story of Jesus's acceptance of death on a cross?
- How does the cross become, as Robb suggests, "our rainbow"?

Optional Activity

At the end of chapter one, Robb discusses *tikkun olam*, the idea of repairing or healing the world. It is a term that is unfamiliar to many Christians. Use this time as an opportunity to draw connections between what Christians see as our calling and its close relationship to Judaism.

- Have you ever thought of your role as a follower of Jesus to involve participating with Christ in the re-creation of God's world? How does this idea affect your understanding of discipleship?
- Why would God entrust fallen human beings with part of the task of healing a world that they helped break?
- Where have you witnessed *tikkun olam* in your life or in your community? How do you connect *tikkun olam* to God's covenant with Noah and creation?

- When have you felt renewed as part of God's creation?
- How does healing of the world involve the kind of trusting relationship that Noah had with God; that Adam and Eve originally had with God; and that Jesus invites us to enter when he tells us to be like the lilies of the field?
- In the spirit of *tikkun olam*, what will you give up for Lent?

Closing Activity

Remind participants that this is a Lenten study—a time when we are called to step out in faith and follow Jesus all the way to the cross. It is also a study when we will dive more deeply into God's work over time in seeking to establish covenant relationships with human beings based on the faith required to follow in response to God's unconditional, unending love.

At the end of each session, ask these two questions:

1. In the coming week, how will you prepare yourself to follow Jesus to the cross?
2. In the past week, when did you notice a reminder of God's love for human beings? Where did you see that love breaking through the barriers we find in our society that separate people from each other?

Close the session with this prayer or one of your own:

Lord, this season reminds us that you never stop trying to reach us with your love, no matter how much we rebel against your plan for the world. Let that love change our hearts so that we have the courage to follow you, to live according to your justice and mercy, and to contribute to the healing of this world in the places where we encounter brokenness. Amen.

Abraham:

A Promise of Nations

Session Goals

This session's reading, discussion, reflection, and prayer will equip participants to:

- Understand what it means to answer God's call to walk by faith rather than by sight;
- Recognize the connection between God's call to Abraham and Jesus's call to his disciples (including us) to "follow me";
- Reflect on how God was faithful to promises and is faithful to us in our own lives;
- Consider how God chooses people for particular roles or tasks;
- Practice living in faith.

Biblical Foundations

When Abram was ninety-nine years old, the LORD appeared to Abram and said to him, "I am God Almighty; walk before me, and be blameless. And I will make my covenant between me and you and will make you exceedingly numerous." Then Abram fell on his face, and God said to him, "As for me, this is my covenant with you: You shall be the ancestor of a multitude of nations. No longer shall your name be Abram, but your name shall be Abraham, for I have made you the ancestor of a multitude of nations. I will make you exceedingly fruitful, and I will make nations of you, and kings shall come from you. I will establish my covenant between me and you and your offspring after you throughout their generations, for an everlasting covenant, to be God to you and to your offspring after you. And I will give to you and to your offspring after you the land where you are now an alien, all the land of Canaan, for a perpetual holding, and I will be their God. . . ."

God said to Abraham, "As for Sarai your wife, you shall not call her Sarai, but Sarah shall be her name. I will bless her and also give you a son by her. I will bless her, and she shall give rise to nations; kings of peoples shall come from her."

(Genesis 17:1-8, 15-16)

Suggested Leader Preparation

- Carefully and prayerfully read this passage and make notes of whatever grabs your attention most and sparks questions or new insights. If desired, consult a trusted Bible commentary.
- Carefully read *Remember: God's Covenants and the Cross*, chapter two. Note any material you need or want to research further before the session.
- Have on hand a variety of Bible translations and trusted study Bibles and commentaries for participants to use (recommended).
- If using the DVD, preview the session two segment and choose the best time in your session to view it.

As Your Group Gathers

Welcome participants. Ask those who attended the previous session to talk briefly about what in it most interested, challenged, or helped them.

Note that this week's discussion centers around the life and feelings of an elderly couple. To better understand and appreciate how Abram and Sarai responded to God's call, invite the group to spend a few moments in silence thinking about elderly people they know (older parents or other relatives, friends)—and how they feel about themselves and their futures. What fears or uncertainties have they faced as they grew older? What emotions did they feel? Did age make them more open to new possibilities or more isolated? What might have spurred them to make dramatic changes in their life circumstances, such as moving to a new city or leaving their home for a senior living community?

Invite participants to share some of these experiences and feelings if they are comfortable in doing so.

Pray this prayer or one in your own words:

Lord, because you are doing new things in the world every day, you continually call us to step out in faith to places we have never been before. You ask us to trust you enough to leave our comfort zones. We remember Jesus's simple invitation to his disciples: "Follow me." Especially during this season of Lent, may we remember how you fulfilled your covenant with Abraham. And may we have the faith and the courage to follow you, even to the cross. Amen.

Answering the Call

In chapter two, Robb emphasizes Abram's remarkable response to a promise that could reasonably be regarded as absurd. He and Sarai are elderly, but they are wealthy and well settled. Abram lacks an heir, but the couple have all the material comforts they wish. Besides, at their age, it's too late to worry about having children.

But when God promises to give Abram a son; and not just a son but descendants; and not just descendants but a great nation to which he will be father; and a new land on top of all that; Abram never questions whether or how this can happen. Unlike so many other figures in the Bible who offer objections when God places a call on them, Abram never raises questions about this ridiculous-sounding promise. He just goes.

Jesus references Abraham in his teaching. Paul makes his case for the primacy of faith on Abraham's example. The writer of Hebrews anchors the most memorable chapter of his long, written sermon (Hebrews 11) on Abraham.

With this in mind, discuss these questions:

- Has there been a time in your life when you have felt, or been, displaced, or had to pick up and move to a new location, town, or country?
- In what ways might you have felt like Abram and Sarai?
- When has God called you to a new place or a new position?
- Did you sense God's guidance in any of that time?
- Did that instance feel like a new birth to you?
- Compare and contrast Abram's response to God's invitation to that of other figures in the Bible:
  ◊ Moses (Exodus 3:7–4:17)
  ◊ Gideon (Judges 6:11-24)
  ◊ Jeremiah (Jeremiah 1:4-12)
  ◊ Barak (Judges 4:1-10)
- Why do you think Abraham stands out compared to all the others?

An Unbelievable Promise

On the face of it, God's promise to Abram sounds unbelievable, even absurd. How are Abram and Sarai, as an eighty-year-old couple, to believe that they not only will have a child, but that this child's descendants will become a great nation who will make Abram's name respected on the earth. Ask participants to discuss:

- Think of a situation when the choice made by a single person made a huge difference in national or world events. Describe that situation to the group.
- When in your life did a choice made by someone make a positive difference in your life? How was it a life-changing moment?

God promises that Abram will be blessed to be a blessing to others. When we are called to step out to some new place in faith, it's easy to focus more on the fear of the unknown instead of the many ways God has blessed us.

Discuss:

- How have you been blessed by God's call(s) in your life?
- In what ways have your blessings blessed others?
- Take stock of the ways God has guided, been present with, and blessed you. How do you feel blessed by God today?

Cutting the Covenant

Robb describes in some detail the ancient Near Eastern ritual that God and Abram perform in "cutting the covenant." Reread Genesis 15:1-19 and discuss these questions:

- What does God do to ratify the covenant? Take careful note of who participates in this ritual. Based on what you read in chapter two, why is this act significant? Why, in your opinion, does only God pass between the two animals and make a pledge on God's life?
- What obligations does God make through the covenant?
- What promises is Abram required to make in this ritual? What does God ask Abram to do?
- How does Abram live into the covenant?
- Because of their advanced age, Abram and Sarai would seem to be odd choices to become the parents of a great nation. But the Scriptures we call the Old Testament are filled with stories of seemingly unlikely people who were chosen by God for special roles. Invite the group to provide examples and describe why these persons were unlikely choices (and, often, themselves were utterly surprised to have been chosen). Some examples include Moses (poor speaking skills, outlaw status in Egypt); Gideon (a fearful man from a small clan, hardly a "mighty warrior" to repel invading enemies); David (small and unimposing). Why might these people also have been the perfect choices for the roles to which God called them?
- Why do you think God may have chosen Abram?

Remembering God's Faithfulness

Abram at times struggles with God's covenant. That's not surprising, given that it takes many years for the son of the promise to be born. Abram might fairly wonder if God's promise will ever come true. Twice, Abram's trust in God appears to waver when he tries to pass off Sarai as his sister instead of his wife. Then, with Sarai's encouragement, Abraham has a son by Sarai's servant, Hagar. As Robb points out, God begins a pattern that will repeat itself throughout these covenant stories by inviting Abram to remember the times God delivered him from possible harm at the hand of the Egyptian pharaoh and a local king; in the face of Abram's wavering and doubts, God remains faithful, encouraging Abram toward continued faithfulness in God. Discuss:

- What are some of the ways you have experienced God's faithfulness in the past?
- When have you experienced doubts in God's faithfulness?
- In what ways, during times of doubt and uncertainty, have you been encouraged to "remember"?
- How does remembering what God has done help you in your journey to the cross through Lent?

A New Name and a New Purpose

At the end of chapter two, Robb connects the new name God gives to Abram, which also signifies the new purpose in his life, to the ritual of Christian baptism, in which we are named before God and the faith community. Have you ever considered that connection? Discuss:

- Review from chapter two how the meaning of Abram's name (meaning "exalted father") changed when he became Abraham (meaning "father of nations").
- Abraham's grandson, Jacob, also received a new name— Israel—from God. Discuss the implications of that name change for both Jacob and his descendants.

- During the ritual of baptism, we are called by name before God. How might this act, particularly when involving the baptism of infants, suggest that God has a purpose for us?
- What does it suggest about the role of the community, which also repeats vows during baptism, about our purpose?

Optional Activity

Say: "In Galatians, the apostle Paul reminds his readers of the story of Abraham to make a point about the paramount importance of faith." Read Galatians 3:6-18 together.

- Ask someone in the group to summarize the argument Paul is making.
- Discuss these questions:
  ◊ Do you agree with Paul's argument?
  ◊ What does Paul's argument suggest about faith in God's covenant promises?
  ◊ In what way does Paul invoke remembrance of God's covenant in communicating to readers who lived eighteen centuries after Abraham's time?

Closing Activity

Remind participants of one of the themes of this Lenten study— that we are called to follow; that we are called to trust in God's promises; and that we are called to remember God's faithfulness. Ask these questions that should be revisited at the end of each session:

- In the coming week, how will you prepare yourself to follow Jesus to the cross?
- In the past week, when did you notice a reminder of God's love for human beings? Where did you see that love breaking through the barriers we find in our society that separate people from each other?

SESSION THREE

Moses and Israel:
Words of Life and Freedom

Session Goals

This session's reading, discussion, reflection, and prayer will equip participants to:

- Recognize new examples in the salvation story of God "remembering" God's people and reaffirming God's promises through a covenant;
- Understand the Ten Commandments not as legalisms but as boundaries that promote life and freedom among God's people;
- Recognize that enslavement can take many forms, including in our own society, and that God's order for the world affirms the liberation of the human body and spirit;
- Help put ourselves in the place of the assembly of Israel at Sinai and feel the wonder and awe of being in God's presence.

Biblical Foundations

"You have seen what I did to the Egyptians and how I bore you on eagles' wings and brought you to myself. Now, therefore, if you obey my voice and keep my covenant, you shall be my treasured possession out of all the peoples. Indeed, the whole earth is mine, but you shall be for me a priestly kingdom and a holy nation."

(Exodus 19:4-6)

Then God spoke all these words:

"I am the LORD *your God, who brought you out of the land of Egypt, out of the house of slavery; you shall have no other gods before me.*

"You shall not make for yourself an idol, whether in the form of anything that is in heaven above or that is on the earth beneath or that is in the water under the earth. You shall not bow down to them or serve them, for I the LORD *your God am a jealous God, punishing children for the iniquity of parents to the third and the fourth generation of those who reject me but showing steadfast love to the thousandth generation of those who love me and keep my commandments.*

"You shall not make wrongful use of the name of the LORD *your God, for the* LORD *will not acquit anyone who misuses his name.*

"Remember the Sabbath day and keep it holy. Six days you shall labor and do all your work. But the seventh day is a Sabbath to the LORD *your God; you shall not do any work—you, your son or your daughter, your male or female slave, your livestock, or the alien resident in your towns. For in six days the* LORD *made heaven and earth, the sea, and all that is in them, but rested the seventh day; therefore the* LORD *blessed the Sabbath day and consecrated it.*

"Honor your father and your mother, so that your days may be long in the land that the LORD *your God is giving you.*

"You shall not murder.

"You shall not commit adultery.

"You shall not steal.

"You shall not bear false witness against your neighbor.

"You shall not covet your neighbor's house; you shall not covet your neighbor's wife, male or female slave, ox, donkey, or anything that belongs to your neighbor."

(Exodus 20:1-17)

Suggested Leader Preparation

- Carefully and prayerfully read Exodus 19:4-6 and Exodus 20:1-17, making notes of whatever grabs your attention most, sparks new questions, or prompts new insights. If desired, consult a trusted Bible commentary. Read also the story of Moses's delivery from the basket set afloat on the Nile (Exodus 2:1-10).

- Carefully read *Remember: God's Covenants and the Cross*, chapter three. Note any material you need or want to research further before the session.
- Have on hand a variety of Bible translations and trusted study Bibles and commentaries for participants to use (recommended). You will need at least two different translations of the Exodus passages that comprise the "Biblical Foundations" for this chapter.
- If using the DVD, preview the session three segment and choose the best time in your session to view it.

As Your Group Gathers

Welcome participants. Ask those who attended the previous session to talk briefly about what in it most interested, challenged, or helped them.

As a way of leading them into this session, invite participants to think about the Ten Commandments. Ask them to list as many of the commandments from memory as they can. (If a whiteboard or large flip chart is available, write down the answers as participants name them.) For each commandment ask:

- What do you think is the purpose of this commandment?
- How does it promote life and freedom for the individual?
- How does it promote life and freedom for the community?
- How does it reflect the broader spirit of the Law?

Pray this prayer or one in your own words:

Lord, in a world where it so often seems that people do as they please, without regard for others, we long for your boundaries that give life and freedom not just to ourselves but to our community. Help us to understand and to live into your covenant, regarding your boundaries not as permission to do anything that stops short of those lines but as words of life that point us toward the spirit of the Law animated by love for you and for all of your children, our neighbors. Amen.

Setting Parental Boundaries

As Robb points out, God is often portrayed in Scripture as a parent. (Note that this is not just characteristic of the Hebrew Scriptures we call the Old Testament; Jesus, too, refers to God in this way.) Those among the participants who are parents will likely have had experience in establishing and enforcing boundaries. God, as a parent, also sets boundaries for human beings, Robb says, "so that we may thrive in the way God intends." Use this background to discuss these questions:

- In what ways do you think of God as a parent?
- How have you experienced God's parenthood in your life?
- How does understanding God as a parent help you better understand the relationship between God and human beings?
- When, as a child or teenager, did your parents set boundaries for you? What were those boundaries intended to accomplish? How, as the child, did you understand and respond to those boundaries?
- What is it about our human nature that seems to lead us to test boundaries?
- Why are boundaries necessary in life?

The Tablets of the Law and the Spirit of the Law

Robb sees to the Ten Commandments as words of life and freedom. Have you ever thought of them in this way, as opposed to restrictions? Discuss:

- In what ways are the Ten Commandments life-giving?
- In what ways do these boundaries actually promote freedom?

- How are these commandments intended to promote benefits to individuals?
- How do they promote life and freedom within the society?
- In your opinion, which benefits—to individuals or to the community—matter most? Why?
- Notice the sequence of the story. God's people do not receive these commandments while they remain enslaved in Egypt. How might these commandments be more appropriate for a people enjoying freedom for the first time in their lives than for people who live under slavery? How do they help them maintain their freedom?
- How have you seen a failure to stay within God's boundaries lead to spiritual and physical consequences that might be described as a form of enslavement?

Robb emphasizes that the laws inscribed on tablets of stone were provided as absolute boundaries, not as rules for which people could seek loopholes. Jesus makes these distinctions clear in his teaching, which focuses on the heart of the Law and spirit of the Law. For example, the Law essentially says: "Whatever else you do, do not murder"; but Jesus says, essentially, that anyone who has desired to injure someone in his or her heart has already violated the Law, even if that desire does not lead to action. With this background in mind, discuss these questions:

- How do you assess the importance of the Ten Commandments, which do not include what Jesus taught were the two greatest commandments (to love God fully and to love our neighbor as ourselves)?
- How do the commandments help us interpret the two greatest commandments?
- Why do you think so much emphasis is placed on displays of the Ten Commandments rather than the two commandments that Jesus emphasized?
- In what ways might the commandments, given to the people while on their journey to the Promised Land of Canaan, represent a moral promised land for their society (and ours)?

Covenants and Remembrance

There's another important aspect to the timing of God's delivery of the covenant at Sinai. It comes *after*—not before—God has liberated the people from slavery in Egypt, and after God provided water and food for the people in the Sinai desert. As Robb notes, God establishes a pattern here that will be repeated over and over through Scripture: God's commandments are prefaced by reminders of what God has done for the people. Because God remembered them, they are to remember to keep God's ordinances that make for life and freedom within the community. Note also for the group that God's covenant is addressed to and made with the entire assembly of Israel, not just with Moses.

- Have you ever thought about the timing for the Ten Commandments in the story of the Israelites' journey in the Sinai wilderness? Why do you think they come after the deliverance from Egypt but before the people enter the Promised Land?
- Why, according to the biblical story, do the people break faith so quickly? What does this suggest to you about the people and their relationship with God?
- What does it suggest about own relationship with God?
- When do we need reminders of what God has done in our lives? When have such reminders helped you through a "wilderness journey"?
- As Robb points out, the mezuzah serves as a reminder of God's commandments for many Jewish people. What memory devices help you within the Christian tradition to remember and be driven by God's faithfulness?
- Compare God's response to the broken covenant by the people with God's reaction to the wickedness in Noah's generation. What, if anything, has changed in God's relationship with the people? in the people's relationship with God?

A Priestly Kingdom and a Holy Nation

Invite participants to review the Biblical Foundations text from Exodus 19. Emphasize that God's stated desire for the people is to be a "priestly kingdom and a holy nation." Then discuss these questions:

- Thinking about the role of priests among the larger group of people, what do you think it means to be a "priestly kingdom"? What does this suggest about how they are to live as God's people? What does it suggest about their relationship to the wider world, which God declares as belonging to God?
- What do you think it meant to be a holy nation in Moses's time?
- What do you think it means to be holy people in a secular society?
- Jesus and the Pharisees often debated about the meaning of this passage. For example, because priests in the Temple washed their hands before eating, the Pharisees in their desire for the people to be a holy nation wanted to impose the same standard on everyone; Jesus insisted that this was not necessary. What, in your mind, defines what it means to be a priestly kingdom and a holy nation?
- During this Lenten season, how will you strive to be a more holy person?

Optional Activity

Read the account of the making of the golden calf from Exodus 32:1-14. Discuss these questions:

- How did the Israelites justify to themselves the making of the golden calf at Mt. Sinai?
- Where did they get all the gold necessary to make the calf?
- How does Aaron explain the making of the calf to Moses?

- In light of Aaron's actions at Sinai, what does it suggest to you that priests among the Israelites are descended from him? What does it suggest about God? What does it suggest about the relationship between God and humans?

Closing Activity

Remind participants of one of the themes of this Lenten study—that we are called to follow; that we are called to trust in God's promises; and that we are called to remember God's faithfulness. Revisit the questions that close each session:

- In the coming week, how will you prepare yourself to follow Jesus to the cross?
- In the past week, when did you notice a reminder of God's love for human beings? Where did you see that love breaking through the barriers we find in our society that separate people from each other?

Close this session by praying these words or some of your own:

O God, we long to feel your presence guiding us as a parent, the way the children of Israel must have felt when they were gathered at the base of Mount Sinai and heard thunder and saw lightning above. Help us to feel your parental hand holding us, protecting us as we grow into the relationship with you and each other that you desire and that your commandments guide us toward. Amen.

David:

An Eternal Covenant

Session Goals

This session's reading, discussion, reflection, and prayer will equip participants to:

- Place themselves in the position of those who first understood God's promise to David as an eternal covenant with the Jewish people;
- Consider how those words would have been understood in David's time and by people of subsequent generations who remembered God's deliverance, God's elevation of the lowly and unpretentious, and God's faithfulness across the centuries;
- Apply this understanding to gain a deeper appreciation of what God's covenant with David means for Christians, who understand Jesus as both the fulfillment of God's promise to continue David's line and the restoration of the original ideal of God as the true king over God's people.

Biblical Foundations

Thus says the LORD of hosts: I took you from the pasture, from following the sheep to be prince over my people Israel, and I have been with you wherever you went and have cut off all your enemies from before you, and I will make for you a great name, like the name of the great ones of the earth. And I will appoint a place for my people Israel and will plant them, so that they may live in their own place and be disturbed no more, and evildoers shall afflict them no more, as formerly, from the time that I appointed judges over my people Israel, and I will give you rest from all your enemies. Moreover, the LORD declares to you that the LORD will make you a house. When your days are fulfilled and you lie down with your ancestors, I will raise up your offspring after you, who shall come forth from your body, and I will establish his kingdom. He shall build a house for my name, and I will establish the throne of his kingdom forever . . . . Your house and your kingdom shall be made sure forever before me; your throne shall be established forever.

(2 Samuel 7:8b-13, 16)

Suggested Leader Preparation

- Carefully and prayerfully read 2 Samuel 7:8-16, making notes of whatever grabs your attention most, sparks new questions, or prompts new insights. If desired, consult a trusted Bible commentary.
- Carefully read *Remember: God's Covenants and the Cross*, chapter four. Note any material you need or want to research further before the session.
- Have on hand a variety of Bible translations and trusted study Bibles and commentaries for participants to use (recommended).
- If using the DVD, preview the session four segment and choose the best time in your session to view it.

As Your Group Gathers

Welcome participants. Ask those who attended the previous session to talk briefly about what in it most interested, challenged, or helped them.

As an opening activity, **say**: "At the beginning of chapter four, Robb invited us to consider what image comes to mind when we think of David. So let's discuss that question together."

- **Ask:** What image comes first into your mind when you think of David? Why?

Allow time for participants to share their answers. Some of the images that participants may mention include:

- Brave boy who killed the giant Goliath
- Ruddy-faced shepherd
- Warrior and conqueror
- Adulterer, plotter, and murderer
- Ancestor of Jesus

If participants did not mention one of these images, mention it to the group and discuss how it adds to their picture of David.

Pray this prayer or one of your own:

Lord, as we prepare our hearts and minds during this Lenten season, we remember your faithfulness as expressed in the covenants with creation, with Abraham, with Moses and the children of Israel, and with David. May the memory of that faithfulness give us the courage and the faith to follow where you call us to go, secure in the knowledge that you are with us and that you keep your promises. Amen.

Remember to Remember

Robb notes that, in the stories in the Bible, when God reminds individuals or groups of what God has done for them, it's a sign that God is preparing to announce a covenant. As we read in chapter four, the pattern from earlier covenants continues with David. Review briefly each of the previous covenants addressed in this book. Discuss:

- What promise did God make to the previous covenant parties?
- What had God done for each of the covenant parties that they were called to remember?
- What promise did God make to David?
- What did God call on David to remember?

- How does remembering become part of God's covenant commitment?
- Thinking back to the earlier covenant parties, why do you think God chose Noah? Abraham? Moses and the people of Israel? David?
- If God were speaking to you as God spoke to these covenant parties, what things do you think God would ask you to remember?

Can We Stand on the Promises?

Say: In his Holocaust memoir, *Night*, Elie Wiesel describes a group of rabbis at Auschwitz who stage a trial and vote to "convict" God of abandoning the covenant with the Jewish people. As evidence, they may have used some of the words from God's promises to David: "evildoers shall afflict [the people] no more"; they "may live in their own place"; "your house and your kingdom shall be made forever secure before me." Discuss:

- How do we interpret God's promise in light of the Babylonian Exile (approximately 400 years after David's time), in light of the destruction of the Temple and the dispersal of the people by the Romans in 70 CE, and in light of the Holocaust?
- How do we know that God remembers?
- When have you felt like those exiled in Babylon? What were your circumstances? Could you finally see that God was with you and loved you amid this dark time? How did that happen?
- In spite of God's promise to him, David had moments when he felt abandoned and all alone—exemplified by the words of Psalm 22 that Jesus quoted from the cross: "My God, my God, why have you forsaken me?" Where do you find assurance that God has not forgotten and forsaken you?

David the Covenant Breaker

As Robb explains, despite everything God has done for him, David fails to keep faith. And he does so in spectacular fashion, violating five of the Ten Commandments—coveting his neighbor's wife, committing adultery, stealing his neighbor's wife, bearing false witness, and committing murder—in the series of actions that result from his lust for Bathsheba. Use this background to discuss the following questions:

- How does the prophet Nathan cause David to remember God's covenants in prompting him to confront his faithlessness?
- How do David's actions create consequences for him and his family?
- What do consequences suggest to you about the covenant relationship between God and the people?
- Why did David's response to being confronted with his sins matter so much to God? How does God respond?
- What does it mean for you as a Christian to confront sin? What does it mean for Christian communities to confront sin?

The Once and Future King

The meaning of God's covenant with David is a point on which Christians and Jews may disagree. To adherents of Judaism in Jesus's time, the promise that a descendant of David, who had been anointed king, would rule over the kingdom was an article of faith (even after the line had been broken with the Babylonian Exile, the prophet Isaiah wrote that God would raise up a new king from "the stump of Jesse" [David's father]). Christians understand Jesus as the Messiah, which means "anointed one." Discuss:

- How was memory of the covenant with David important to Matthew and Luke, who trace the genealogy of Jesus at the beginning of their Gospels?
- How, according to Robb, did Jesus fulfill the covenant with David in an unexpected way?
- How, in the Christian understanding, did the arrival of Jesus allow God to restore an earlier relationship with the people of Israel? How did it represent a new chapter in God's relationship with the entire world?

- When have you seen God act in ways you had not expected? How did you (and others) react initially to this unexpected behavior? Was it difficult for you to recognize? Was it difficult to accept? Did your reaction change over time? How?

Optional Activity

Read all of Psalm 22 and Psalm 23 aloud for the group.

Say: "These are both psalms associated with David. Some of you may have memorized Psalm 23 as children. We know the opening words of Psalm 22 in part because Jesus quotes them from the cross."

Discuss these questions:

- Compare and contrast the tone and feel of each psalm.
- How could two psalms that express such different emotional states reflect the faith of the same author (David)?
- How does the tone of Psalm 22 change as you read the entire text? How does the author remember God's promises and faithfulness?
- How does Psalm 23 reflect the memory of God's promises and faithfulness?

Closing Activity

As you prepare to end this session, read together Psalm 51:1-17:

Have mercy on me, O God,
*   according to your steadfast love;*
according to your abundant mercy,
*   blot out my transgressions.*
Wash me thoroughly from my iniquity,
*   and cleanse me from my sin.*

For I know my transgressions,
*   and my sin is ever before me.*
Against you, you alone, have I sinned
*   and done what is evil in your sight,*
so that you are justified in your sentence
*   and blameless when you pass judgment.*

Indeed, I was born guilty,
  a sinner when my mother conceived me.

You desire truth in the inward being;
  therefore teach me wisdom in my secret heart.
Purge me with hyssop, and I shall be clean;
  wash me, and I shall be whiter than snow.
Let me hear joy and gladness;
  let the bones that you have crushed rejoice.
Hide your face from my sins,
  and blot out all my iniquities.

Create in me a clean heart, O God,
  and put a new and right spirit within me.
Do not cast me away from your presence,
  and do not take your holy spirit from me.
Restore to me the joy of your salvation,
  and sustain in me a willing spirit.

Then I will teach transgressors your ways,
  and sinners will return to you.
Deliver me from bloodshed, O God,
  O God of my salvation,
  and my tongue will sing aloud of your deliverance.

O Lord, open my lips,
  and my tongue will declare your praise.
For you have no delight in sacrifice;
  if I were to give a burnt offering, you would not be pleased.
The sacrifice acceptable to God is a broken spirit;
  a broken and contrite heart, O God, you will not despise.

Say: The note in the Bible that accompanies Psalm 51 tells us David composed these verses after being confronted by Nathan over his sin with Bathsheba and the murder of her husband, Uriah. During Lent, we are called to confront our own sin and brokenness. Discuss:

- How does memory of God's response to the brokenness of others in our salvation story contribute to your faith and your willingness to follow Jesus?

- How does confession help you build stronger relationships with others?

Remind participants of one of the themes of this Lenten study—that we are called to follow, that we are called to trust in God's promises, and that we are called to remember God's faithfulness. Revisit the questions that close each session:

- In the coming week, how will you prepare yourself to follow Jesus to the cross?
- In the past week, when did you notice a reminder of God's love for human beings? Where did you see that love breaking through the barriers we find in our society that separate people from each other?

Pray this prayer or one of your own:

Lord, during this season as we attempt to follow Jesus to the cross, we remember that you have promised to be always with us, that nothing can separate us from your love, and that when we bring our brokenness to you, you promise to put it aside as far as the east is from the west. May these assurances give us strength and faith for our journey with Jesus.

From Jeremiah to Jesus:
The Covenant of the Heart

Session Goals

This session's reading, discussion, reflection, and prayer will equip participants to:

- Place themselves in the position of the prophet Jeremiah as he witnessed the people break faith with God in ways that were profoundly shocking to him and signified a complete rebellion against God's intended order;
- Appreciate how, in light of this rebellion, Jeremiah's announcement of a new covenant, to be written the people's hearts, represented an act of "amazing grace" and signified God's unmistakable intent to be in a loving and intimate relationship with the people in spite of their rebellion;
- Recognize how our own society may create Gehennas—places that exemplify a willful turning away from God and the elevation or even worship of false gods.

Biblical Foundations

The days are surely coming, says the LORD, when I will make a new covenant with the house of Israel and the house of Judah. It will not be like

the covenant that I made with their ancestors when I took them by the hand
to bring them out of the land of Egypt—a covenant that they broke, though
I was their husband, says the LORD. But this is the covenant that I will
make with the house of Israel after those days, says the LORD: I will put my
law within them, and I will write it on their hearts; and I will be their God,
and they shall be my people. No longer shall they teach one another or say
to each other, "Know the LORD," for they shall all know me, from the least
of them to the greatest, says the LORD; for I will forgive their iniquity and
remember their sin no more.

(Jeremiah 31:31-34)

Suggested Leader Preparation

- Carefully and prayerfully read Jeremiah 31:31-34, making
  notes of whatever grabs your attention most, sparks new
  questions, or prompts new insights. If desired, consult a trusted
  Bible commentary.
- Carefully read *Remember: God's Covenants and the Cross*,
  chapter five. Note any material you need or want to research
  further before the session.
- Have on hand a variety of Bible translations and trusted
  study Bibles and commentaries for participants to use
  (recommended).
- If using the DVD, preview the session five segment and choose
  the best time in your session to view it.
- Read some background on the practice of child sacrifice in
  ancient Israel and the Valley of the Son of Hinnom.

As Your Group Gathers

Welcome participants. Ask those who attended the previous
session to talk briefly about what in it most interested, challenged, or
helped them.

Invite the group to share "covenant sightings" from the past week—
times when they were reminded of God's faithfulness in human affairs.

Then invite the group to share how remembering these moments
of faithfulness helped them on their journey through the week.

Pray this prayer or one of your own:

Lord, as we follow Jesus during this Lenten season, give us the spirit to hear the prophetic voices in our midst who remind us that we have turned away from you. Give us the spirit to repent and return to you. And let us be receptive to your love that your law and your precepts may be written on our hearts. Amen.

Your Personal Freeway Moments

In chapter five, Robb recounts a time when she experienced a sharp and jarring realization, while driving on a freeway, that she had turned away from God. Invite participants to share their own experiences when they believed that God was sending a message to them about their spiritual lives or a calling that God had placed on them. Invite participants to share their own "freeway moments"—times when they realized they had fallen away from God and that God was trying to reach them. Discuss:

- Why do you think the shepherds were afraid by the appearance of the angels? Why do you think that the angels deemed it necessary, in their encounters with Mary, Joseph, Elizabeth, Zechariah (and, later, the women who came to the tomb on Easter morning) to reassure them that they need not be afraid?
- Why do you think our initial impulse to something unexpected is fear? How is that impulse helpful? How can it be harmful?
- Can you think of a time when you were terrified to receive news that turned out to be good? Describe it.
- How can fear hold us back from experiencing something new and amazing?

The Role of Prophets, Then and Now

In the Hebrew Scriptures that we call the Old Testament, prophets filled an important role. The word *prophet* means "one who speaks for

God." The prophetic role was less about predicting the future than about speaking on God's behalf about the state of things in their own time. More specifically, prophets reminded the people of God's standards of love, fidelity, and justice and pointed out to people how they were not living up to those standards. Read several passages from the Old Testament in which prophets deliver a message from God about the behavior of the people:

- Isaiah 58 (true worship)
- Amos 5 (idol worship, true worship)
- Amos 8:4-10 (selling the poor for a pair of sandals)
- Hosea 4:12-19 (idol worship)
- Isaiah 1:10-23 (widows and orphans)
- Jeremiah 7:30-34 (Hinnom)

For each of these passages, discuss:

- What message was the prophet attempting to deliver? Where had the people fallen short of God's expectations? How had they broken faith with God's intended order?
- How did these prophets call on the people to "remember"?

Then discuss these questions:

- In chapter five, Robb mentions Jesus's parable of the wicked tenants. Who in that story fulfilled the role of prophets? How did they speak for God? What response did they receive?
- What does it mean to speak with "the prophetic voice"?
- Where in our society today do you hear the prophetic voice?

Making Our Gehennas

In chapter five of *Remember: God's Covenants and the Cross*, Robb describes sacrifices of children to pagan gods at the place near Jerusalem known as the Valley of the Son of Hinnom—and relates how this place gave us the word *Gehenna* that Jesus uses to describe an eternal place of separation from God. Because Gehenna was a place that human beings, not God, created, in using this image Jesus appears to be suggesting that separation from God is a human choice, not God's choice, and that this choice has consequences both in the present and for all time. With this as background, discuss the following questions together:

- Where in our society today do you find examples of idolatry—putting man-made things or human values above steadfast and complete love for God? What makes them idolatrous?
- Many people in Jeremiah's time had a blind spot about idol worship, rationalizing it away as harmless and failing to recognize that it was incompatible with loyalty to God. Do you think people have blind spots today about the examples of idolatry participants identified in the preceding question?
- How have these examples of modern-day idolatry helped bring about modern-day Gehennas in our society? What harmful consequences have they created?

As Robb notes, Jesus invokes the imagery of Gehenna in his parable of the rich man and Lazarus the beggar. Read this parable from Luke 16 and discuss these questions:

- Why does Lazarus wind up after his death being comforted in the bosom of Abraham?
- In the story, what do you think Abraham meant when he castigated the rich man for surrounding himself with "worthless things"?
- How do the rich man's choices in life determine his ultimate fate? How was that fate something that he constructed for himself?
- How, in Jesus's teaching, was the rich man guilty of idolatry like those who originally built altars at Gehenna?
- How, at the end of the parable, were the rich man's father and brothers called to "remember"?

The Days Are Surely Coming

The text for chapter five of *Remember: God's Covenants and the Cross* comes from Jeremiah 31. After the prophet has denounced the rulers and people of Judah for worshipping idols and forsaking God, we read the astonishing promise that Jeremiah makes on God's behalf: Even though the people broke the covenant, even though they rebelled in ways that were abhorrent to God, God is going to set these offenses aside and make a new covenant. Discuss the meaning and implications of this covenant through these questions:

- What does it suggest about God's nature that God would simply replace the covenant that humans repeatedly broke with a new covenant?
- What does it suggest about God's desire for a close and trusting relationship with human beings?
- How does a covenant written on the heart differ from a covenant written in books or etched in stone? How does it contribute to your understanding of what it means to abide by the terms of the covenant?
- Where do you see parallels between Jeremiah's "covenant of the heart" and Jesus's teaching that the condition of one's heart is as important to outward adherence to the written commandments of the Law?
- When Jesus forgives his killers even as he is dying on the cross, saying that they do not realize what they are doing, where do you hear echoes of Jeremiah's new covenant?

Optional Activity

Using their cell phones, invite participants to view the text of Dr. Martin Luther King's "I Have a Dream" speech. Invite participants to skim through the text and identify the two quotations used by Dr. King from the Hebrew prophets:

Let justice roll down like water,
   and righteousness like an ever-flowing stream.
                    (Amos 5:24)

"Every valley shall be lifted up,
   and every mountain and hill be laid low;
the uneven ground shall become level,
   and the rough places a plain."
                    (Isaiah 40:4)

Consulting your Bibles (either have copies on hand or invite participants to use their phones), look up the chapters in which these two passages occur. Discuss:

- What is the context of these passages in the message of these two prophets?
- What is the context that Dr. King applies to these passages?
- How did Dr. King adopt the prophetic tradition in delivering a message to the nation on that summer day in 1963?
- Do you see Dr. King as a prophet in our own society, like Amos, Isaiah, and Jeremiah? If so, in what way?
- Where do you see the prophetic voice being proclaimed today in our society?

Closing Activity

Remind participants of one of the themes of this Lenten study—that we are called to follow, that we are called to trust in God's promises, and that we are called to remember God's faithfulness. Revisit the questions that close each session:

- In the coming week, how will you prepare yourself to follow Jesus to the cross?
- In the past week, when did you notice a reminder of God's love for human beings? Where did you see that love breaking through the barriers we find in our society that separate people from each other?

Pray this prayer or one of your own:

Lord, when we are reminded of how we have fallen away from you, we also remember your willingness to make a new covenant to replace the one that we broke—and your promise that it would be forever written on our hearts. We are overwhelmed by your amazing grace that would set aside even our worst offenses. Help us to respond to your forgiveness by teaching others, as your prophet foretold, and by building communities around your love, your justice, and your mercy. Amen.

SESSION SIX

Jesus and the New Covenant

Session Goals

This session's reading, discussion, reflection, and prayer will equip participants to:

- Place themselves in the position of the disciples who gathered with Jesus for what they would later remember as their final meal together;
- Connect Jesus's language, in which he says his blood represents a renewal of the covenant, with previous covenants;
- Understand Jesus's invitation to act "in remembrance of me" as a call to remember what Jesus is about to do as a model for self-giving love;
- Understand the cross, like the rainbow in the time of Noah, as an eternal sign that human death and violence have no power to prevent God's love from reaching us—or to prevent us from coming home at last to God.

Biblical Foundations

He said to them, "I have eagerly desired to eat this Passover with you before I suffer, for I tell you, I will not eat it until it is fulfilled in the kingdom of God." Then he took a cup, and after giving thanks he said, "Take this and divide it among yourselves, for I tell you that from now on

*I will not drink of the fruit of the vine until the kingdom of God comes."
Then he took a loaf of bread, and when he had given thanks he broke it
and gave it to them, saying, "This is my body, which is given for you.
Do this in remembrance of me." And he did the same with the cup after
supper, saying, "This cup that is poured out for you is the new covenant
in my blood."*

(Luke 22:15-20)

*For I received from the Lord what I also handed on to you, that the Lord
Jesus on the night when he was betrayed took a loaf of bread, and when he
had given thanks, he broke it and said, "This is my body that is [broken]
for you. Do this in remembrance of me." In the same way he took the cup
also, after supper, saying, "This cup is the new covenant in my blood.
Do this, as often as you drink it, in remembrance of me." For as often as
you eat this bread and drink the cup, you proclaim the Lord's death until
he comes.*

(1 Corinthians 11:23-26)

Suggested Leader Preparation

- Carefully and prayerfully read Luke 22:15-20 and
  1 Corinthians 11:23-26, making notes of whatever grabs
  your attention most, sparks new questions, or prompts new
  insights. If desired, consult a trusted Bible commentary.
- Carefully read *Remember: God's Covenants and the Cross*,
  chapter six. Note any material you need or want to research
  further before the session.
- Have on hand a variety of Bible translations and trusted
  study Bibles and commentaries for participants to use
  (recommended).
- If using the DVD, preview the session six segment and choose
  the best time in your session to view it.

As Your Group Gathers

Welcome participants. Ask those who attended the previous
session to talk briefly about what in it most interested, challenged, or
helped them.

If feasible, arrange the group around a large table for this session, which will focus on Jesus and his disciples around a table on their last night together.

Invite the group to share "covenant sightings" from the past week—times when they were reminded of God's faithfulness in human affairs.

Then invite the group to share how remembering these moments of faithfulness helped them on their journey through the week.

Pray this prayer or one of your own:

Lord, we remember how you invite us to gather around you together, the way your disciples gathered around the table and shared a meal. Especially in this season, make us mindful of what you prayed for them—that we be one in faith, one in love, one in spirit, and one in following you. Amen.

Rebooting the Covenant

At the beginning of chapter six, Robb writes about her occasional frustration with technology, such as her laptop computer or cell phone—and the need to reboot and start again. She goes on to apply the need for rebooting to human relationships and to the covenant relationship between God and human beings.

Invite participants to place their cell phones on the table in front of them.

- Ask how many have rebooted their phones in the preceding week. If so, why did they need to reboot? What did the reboot accomplish?
- How did the reboot affect the relationship between the user and the phone?
- How does the idea of rebooting apply to human relationships? Invite members of the group to share experiences, either their own or involving others, when they have witnessed a rebooted relationship between people.
- What does it take to accomplish a rebooted relationship between people? Specifically, what did it take from the person

who initiated the reboot? What did it take from the person who responded to the invitation to a rebooted relationship?

- How is the idea of a reboot applicable to the "salvation story" that we have examined throughout *Remember: God's Covenants and the Cross*?
- What did it take from God to initiate the covenant reboots we have examined in this book? What did it take from humans to respond?
- How does Jesus initiate a covenant reboot during the Last Supper?
- How do the cross and the Resurrection represent a reboot of the covenant?

Around the Table

In chapter six, Robb brings us to the table where Jesus and his disciples shared their last supper together. She notes how our memories often take us back to own family times around a table sharing a meal.

- Invite participants to share some of their own memories of family meal traditions (which may involve both special occasions or everyday routines).

Say: "According to the Synoptic Gospels—Matthew, Mark, and Luke—Jesus and his disciples share a Passover meal on their last night together. According to John's Gospel, the last supper occurred the day before Passover, when lambs were being slaughtered across the land in preparation for Passover rituals. Either way, this was a meal that took place during a holiday week, much as families gather together for festive meals at Thanksgiving and Christmastime." Discuss:

- In what ways was the Last Supper like a family gathering for a meal?
- What was the significance, in your opinion, of identifying this as a Passover meal, as the Synoptic Gospels do?

- What was the significance of situating this meal on the day before Passover, when lambs were being sacrificed, as John does?
- For Jesus's disciples, how would either of these dates for the Last Supper connect to "remembering" God's actions on behalf of their ancestors?
- What does it suggest to you that even Judas was included in the final meal, even though Jesus knew he was about to betray him? What does it suggest about inclusion and exclusion in our own lives? In the lives of our Christian communities?
- How does the experience of Holy Communion today connect you to what Robb calls "God's covenantal family"?
- How does remembering together contribute to your willingness to follow in faith toward the place that God will show us?

One of Us

In chapter six of *Remember: God's Covenants and the Cross*, Robb relates a story told by the late Paul Harvey about a man who wishes he could become a bird in order to show a group of birds the way to safety during a dangerous blizzard. Use that story to discuss these questions as a group:

- How does Robb relate this story to the incarnation and life of Jesus?
- **Say:** "As Christians, we frequently talk about the consequences for human beings of God's decision to live, through Jesus, as a human being. We talk less often about the consequences for God." Ask:
  ◊ What might God have experienced directly as a human being that God might not have experienced without entering the world through Jesus? What emotions? What pain?

◊ Why do you think God would feel a need or desire to experience life and death as a human being? What does this act suggest to you about God's nature and being?

◊ How does the Incarnation play into the idea of a covenant reboot?

- **Say:** "Once Jesus was born as a human being, his human death became an inevitability. The only question was what type of human death he would experience." Ask:

◊ Why would God choose to experience a human death that involved the kind of pain, agony, humiliation, and loneliness involved in a crucifixion?

◊ Why do you think God might allow God's self to be subjected to the ability of human beings to inflict punishment and death—particularly a type of death that involved the exercise of state power?

- **Say:** "Especially in the millennium after Jesus's life, Christians often referred to Jesus not only as our Lord and our Savior but as our brother." Ask:

◊ Why would Christians think of Jesus as a brother?

◊ How does this contribute to your understanding of Jesus as "one of us"?

The Old/New Covenant

In chapter six of *Remember: God's Covenants and the Cross*, Robb notes how the Gospel writers (and the apostle Paul) do not uniformly agree about whether the Last Supper was a Passover meal and whether, in describing "my covenant," Jesus used the adjective "new." She observes how, during this final meal with the disciples, Jesus invokes a concept from earlier covenants between God and humans: ratification with blood. She also suggests that the "new" covenant, instituted amid a meal around a table, "was the beginning of a new life, a new direction, and a new identity for the disciples, for the church, and for us."

With this as context, discuss:

- How does Jesus's invocation of the shedding of blood take us back to God's promises in the earlier covenants made with Abraham and Moses and the children of Israel? How does the shedding of Jesus's own blood add to your understanding of these earlier covenants?

- How does the cross represent the beginning of a new covenant?

- **Say:** "In previous covenants, as Robb notes, God invites human beings to remember what God has done for them, using these remembrances as reasons to have faith that God will keep covenant promises." Ask:

  ◊ What promises, explicitly or implicitly, does Jesus offer to his followers (including us) through the new covenant?

  ◊ What reasons does Jesus give to have faith in these promises?

- Do you believe it is possible to separate the cross from the Resurrection as part of this new covenant? Is it possible to separate Jesus's sacrifice on our behalf from the promise, made manifest through the Resurrection, that we, like Jesus, can "overcome the world"? Why or why not?

- In what ways do Jesus's death and resurrection remind you of God's original invitation to Abram to follow in faith "to the land that I will show you"?

- Why, in your opinion, do New Testament writers like the apostle Paul (Galatians 3:6-9, 16-18) and the writer of the Letter to the Hebrews (11:8-12) remind their readers of Abraham's example when encouraging them to follow Jesus? [*As group leader, you may find it helpful to read these passages together as a group in discussing this question.*]

- How does Abraham's example help you on your own faith journey?

- **Say:** "Robb suggests that, if we're honest with ourselves, we find ourselves at the cross alongside Jesus's killers, confronting our own brokenness and betrayal." Ask:

  ◊ How does this self-honesty contribute to our understanding of the depth of God's love?

  ◊ How does it contribute to our understanding of the new covenant ratified by Jesus's death and resurrection?

  ◊ How does it change the way we relate to other human beings?

Optional Activity

Bring Communion elements, bread and grape juice, to your gathering and keep them on the table around which the group has gathered. If an ordained pastor is not part of your study group, you may ask the pastor to consecrate the elements in advance of your gathering.

Before your closing activity, read aloud the earliest account of Jesus's last supper with his disciples (1 Corinthians 11:23-26).

Share the bread and the cup with each other around the table. If possible, have one loaf of bread and one chalice with grape juice. Allow each person to break off a piece of the loaf as it is passed from one participant to the next. In passing the bread, each person should say in turn: "This is the body of Christ, given for you." Then, passing the cup, invite participants likewise to say: "This is the blood of Christ, given for you." Have participants dip their piece of bread into the juice and eat.

Say: "As Paul understood and taught, when we partake of the bread and the cup, in remembrance of Jesus's sacrifice for us, we also remember how Christ makes us one body. Because Christ is at work within us, incorporated into our very being, and because Christ is indivisible, then we, too, become joined together like the various parts of one human body. In remembrance of the covenant ratified by Jesus on the night before his death, let us be one with Christ and one with each other, with his self-giving love as our model and our example."

Closing Activity

Remind participants of one of the themes of this Lenten study—that we are called to follow, that we are called to trust in God's promises, and that we are called to remember God's faithfulness. Revisit the questions that close each session:

- In the coming week, how will you prepare yourself to follow Jesus to the cross?
- In the past week, when did you notice a reminder of God's love for human beings? Where did you see that love breaking through the barriers we find in our society that separate people from each other?

Remind participants of John Wesley's famous prayer, known as the Wesleyan Covenant Prayer. According to Wesley's journal, the prayer was first recited in London in 1755, at a service attended by 1,800 people in the Methodist movement. The words are understood as a response to God's grace at work in our lives—our obligations, as Wesley put it, in "renewing the covenant with God."

Close the study by inviting participants to pray these words together, remembering God's faithfulness in our lives and our commitment to be disciples:

I am no longer my own, but thine.
Put me to what thou wilt, rank me with whom thou wilt.
Put me to doing, put me to suffering.
Let me be employed by thee, or laid aside for thee,
exalted for thee or brought low for thee.
Let me be full, let me be empty.
Let me have all things, let me have nothing.

Remember: Leader Guide

> *I freely and wholeheartedly yield all things*
> *to thy pleasure and disposal.*
> *And now, O glorious and blessed God,*
> *Father, Son, and Holy Spirit,*
> *thou art mine and I am thine. So be it.*
> *And the covenant which I have made on earth,*
> *let it be ratified in heaven. Amen.*[1]

---

1   "A Covenant in the Wesleyan Tradition," *The United Methodist Hymnal* (Nashville: The United Methodist Publishing House, 1989), 607

www.ingramcontent.com/pod-product-compliance
Lightning Source LLC
Chambersburg PA
CBHW010858090426
42737CB00020B/3420